"Gabriel Rosenstock is one of the most original, untypical, and inventive writers/thinkers/poets in the world. Within the haiku fraternity, he is unique in the eyes of this reviewer."

-World Haiku Review

Ag Críost an mhuir, ag Críost an t-iasc;
i líonta Dé go gcastar sinn.

(To Christ the sea, to Christ the fish;
May we be together in the nets of God)

From the popular Irish hymn Ag Críost an Síol (To Christ the Seed), music by Seán Ó Riada. The words are said to be by the legendary Co. Clare priest Fr. Mícheál Ó Míocháin (1810-1878)

Haiku in Irish by Gabriel Rosenstock
Transcreated in English by Garry Bannister
Artwork (in Public Domain): Amaldus Nielsen

© Gabriel Rosenstock 2025
Layout by Mandy Marcus
ISBN 978-1-918058-11-6

CRÍOST, IMITHE AG IASCAIREACHT
CHRIST, GONE FISHING

Gabriel Rosenstock

scamaill dhonnrua
Críost imithe ag iascaireacht
lena chairde

russet clouds
Christ gone fishing
with His buddies

níos uaisle
ná teampaill uile an domhain
tigh feirme in Balestrand

    finer
    than all the temples of the world
    a farmhouse in Balestrand *

*Trá cois chnocán an fhéir is brí le hainm an tsráidbhaile. A beach by a little grassy hill explains the name of the village.

nach lán
atá sé!
an folús seo . . .

how full
it is
this void . . .

Críost, fánaí,
is minic a chosa á bhfuarú
anseo aige

*Christ, wanderer,
often here
he cools His feet*

glaonn sé ar an maidin:
dúisigh! dúisigh!
is é solas an tsaoil é

> *He calls out to the morning:*
> *awake! awake!*
> *the light of this world*

an féidir
aon ní fónta
a theacht as sin?

> *could*
> *anything good*
> *come out of this?**

*John.1:46 ("Can anything good come out of there?")

spéir agus uisce
líonta d'ór
cad atá ag teastáil ón duine?

sky and water
filled with gold
what is it men seek?

tráthnóna gleoite!
a shúil ar an ngealbhan
a shúil ar an iasc

a glorious afternoon!
his eye on the sparrow
his eye on the fish*

*Tá a Shúil ar an nGealbhan (1905), iomann gaspal scríofa ag Civilla D. Martin. Charles H. Gabriel a chum an ceol.

His Eye Is on the Sparrow (1905), gospel hymn written by Civilla D. Martin and composer Charles H. Gabriel.

cúr ag éirí
briathra mistéireacha
á bhfoirmiú sa chroí

foam rising
mysterious words
forming in the heart

sléibhte
an gan chúis
atáid?

> *mountains*
> *are they*
> *without a cause?*

á tumadh féin go hurramach
san uisce
abhlann

    submerging itself reverently
    in water
    a wafer

cé atá chugainn?
an Samárach Maith
nó a mhalairt?

> *who comes our way*
> *the Good Samaritan*
> *or someone else?*

clapsholas . . .
déithe agus déithe nach ann dóibh
ag dul chun suain

      twilight . . .
      gods – and imagined gods –
      fall asleep

beanna arda
an Briathar amháin a mhairfdh
dá n-éis

high peaks
only the Word
will survive

Vide: Matha 24:35
***See:** Matthew 24.35*

is scáthanna sinn
ag breathnú amach
ar an bhfarraige

we are shadows
gazing out
to sea

cé a chruthaíonn an calm
cé a líonann na seolta
lena anáil?

who creates the calm
who fills the sails
with His breath?

fuineadh gréine
Íosa ag smaoineamh
ar an mbean rua

sunset
Jesus is thinking
about the red-haired woman*

*Is ina bean rua a léirítear Máire Mhaigdiléana de ghnáth.
*Mary Magdalene is usually depicted as a redhead.

néalta dúigh . . .
is leor mar chomharthaí iontais
sa spéir iad

    inky clouds
    as signs of wonder in the sky
    they suffice

teagasc
agus brainsí uile na giúise
is Aon iad

the teachings
and all the branches of the pine
are One

níl ann ach samhlaíocht file –
long phéinteáilte
ar aigéan péinteáilte

> *it's nothing but a poet's fancy*
> *painted ship*
> *on a painted ocean**

*The Rime of the Ancient Mariner (1834), Coleridge

uaireanta téann sé amach leis féin
tugann seans eile
do mhionéisc

sometimes He goes out on his own
gives another chance
to the smaller fish

is í a bhád siúd í
agus faoileán
á gardáil

His boat it is
a seagull
guarding it

is beag nár chuir iontais Dé
amú iad
Íosa agus a chompánaigh

the wonders of God
almost led them astray
Jesus and his companions

"a Mháistir – cad faoin domhan seo!
nach bhfuil éalú ar bith
ón tsíoraíocht?"

"Master – what of this world!
is there no escape
from eternity?"

eisean a chruthaigh na troill
agus an t-aos sí –
is ní ghéilleann sé dóibh!

He who created trolls
and the fairy folk
He doesn't believe in them!

tráthnónta fada samhraidh
a ghrá á leathnú
ar fud na bhfud

long summer afternoons
His love spreading
far and wide

filíocht na bhfáithe
tine gheal
i seomra folamh

poetry of the prophets
a bright fire
in an empty room

níl siollaí ann
a cheansódh inniu í –
farraige shuaite

*there are no syllables
to calm her today –
troubled sea*

an é féin atá ann –
a chruthaigh gach saghas síne –
amuigh faoin mbáisteach!

is it Himself –
who created every kind of weather –
out under the rain!

tá Ríocht na bhFlaitheas in acmhaireacht . . .
Í Bhreasail?
hath! i bhfad i gcéin

the Kingdom of Heaven is at hand . . .
Hy-Brasil?*
a long way off!

*Phantom island in Gaelic legend.

sinne
na daoine stuáilte . . .
déan trócaire orainn

filled with straw
we are . . .
have mercy on us

Vide: The Hollow Men (1925) de chuid T. S. Eliot
See: The Hollow Men (1925) by T. S. Eliot

leis féin
lena chinniúint . . .
piobaireachd na bóchna

on His own
with his fate . . .
and the pibroch of oceans

Gabriel Rosenstock is a poet, tankaist, haikuist, children's author, novelist, translator, short story writer and in the words of Hugh MacDiarmid, 'a champion of forlorn causes' He has collaborated with Kashmiri artist Masood Hussain on numerous projects such as *Walk with Gandhi* (Free Kids Books), picture books for children, *The Hen/An Chearc* (bilingual edition from Lulu), *Love Letter to Kashmir* (Cross-Cultural Communications, New York), *Boatman! take these songs from me* (Manipal Universal Press, India). *An Cosán* and *The Path* are contemplative, humorous picture books for older children (Cross-Cultural Communications, New York).

He was given the Irish Children's Books Annual Award in 2023 as an acknowledgement of his collections of verse for children and an Arts Council Bursary in 2024 to enable him to add to that growing body of work.

Garry Bannister spent decades preparing his *Téasáras Gaeilge-Béarla/Irish English Thesaurus* (New Island 2023). He studied Irish and Russian in Trinity College, Dublin and set up the first Department of Modern Irish at Moscow State University. On his return to Ireland, he was head of the Irish Department of St. Columba's College. He has transcreated Zen koans into Irish in *A Path Home/Conair Siar* (New Island) and Gabriel Rosenstock's book-length selection of poems which honour a little-known T'ang Dynasty poet, *Comhrá le Lí Hè/Conversations with Li He* (Cross-Cultural Communications, New York, 2021).

Note from the Author, Gabriel Rosenstock:

Allow me to make a confession. I do not have a 'personal', religious, spiritual or mystical relationship with Christ. Never had. I do not know Him from Adam, if the truth be told. And yet some of the haiku and senryu in this book belie such a blatant denial, as does the bilingual book of Christian contemplative ekphrastic haiku *Iontas na nIontas* (2023).

    I am a Catholic by upbringing. Historically, my sympathies would be with the Catholic cause, in the face of the centuries-long relentless colonialism which weaponised Protestantism and the English tongue in its global, imperial outreach, starting with Ireland.

    Irish poets and mystics worked with passion and vision for the freedom we enjoy today, many of them with an unalloyed love of Jesus. The majority of these are unknown to the world at large as they belong to the Gaelic tradition.

    Their modern equivalents rose up in Easter 1916, as though the risen Christ Himself stood behind the risen nation:

> *I see his blood upon the rose*
> *And in the stars the glory of his eyes,*
> *His body gleams amid eternal snows,*
> *His tears fall from the skies.*
>
> *I see his face in every flower;*
> *The thunder and the singing of the birds*
> *Are but his voice – and carven by his power*
> *Rocks are his written words.*
>
> *All pathways by his feet are worn,*
> *His strong heart stirs the ever-beating sea,*
> *His crown of thorns is twined with every thorn,*
> *His cross is every tree.*

Joseph Mary Plunkett

Those insurrectionists, men and women, were Irish-language enthusiasts for the most part. Plunkett was no exception. He was also an Esperantist which tells us that many of the insurrectionists weren't the narrow-minded nationalists sadly depicted by their detractors. Their outlook was broad, universal. P. H. Pearse, in many respects their leader, communicated with Rabindranath Tagore and the Bengali's educational ideas in Shantiniketan found echoes in Pearse's own school, St. Enda's.

Plunkett might have appreciated my Irish-language transcreation of his poem:

> *An fhuil is léir dom ar an rós,*
> *I ngach aon réalt tá glóir a shúl.*
> *Mar shneachta a cholainn, is ritheann fós*
> *A dheora geala ón spéir anuas.*
>
> *Is léir a ghnúis i ngach aon bhláth,*
> *An toirneach agus scol gach éin*
> *A ghuth, ar ndóigh – is snoite tá*
> *A chumhacht sa charraig féin.*
>
> *Is é a shiúil gach cosán dearg,*
> *A chroí a bhogann an tonn tuile,*
> *Fíodh a choróin as gach aon dealg*
> *A chros is beo i ngach aon bhile.*

These words, in either language, do not ring loudly in the hearts of our neo-colonial citizenry today, alas. Everyone in Ireland knows of the 1916 poets, Pearse, Plunkett, McDonagh. A figure of international standing among them was Roger Casement. Ask people do they know of Casement's mystic paeon to the Irish language, and they will look at you askance. Casement? A poet? An Irish-language enthusiast?

The Irish Language

It is gone from the hill and the glen —
The strong speech of our sires;
It is sunk in the mire and the fen
Of our nameless desires:
We have bartered the speech of the Gael
For a tongue that would pay,
And we stand with the lips of us pale
And all bloodless to-day;
We have bartered the birthright of men
That our sons should be liars.
It is gone from the hill and the glen,
The strong speech of our sires.
Like the flicker of gold on the whin
That the Spring breath unites,
It is deep in our hearts, and shall win
Into flame where it smites:
It is there with the blood in our veins,
With the stream in the glen,
With the hill and the heath and the weans
They shall think *it again;*
It shall surge to their lips and shall win
The high road to our rights —
Like the flicker of gold on the whin
That the sun-burst unites.

Such high idealism is hard to find in today's Ireland. (There may be a hint of that in **Haiku 27** which suggests that prophetic words fall on deaf ears). I was emboldened by Casement's little-known poem to transcreate it in Irish:

An Teanga Ghaeilge

Do thréig sí an cnoc is an gleann
teanga thréan na sean;
Sa láib di seachas ar an mbeann –
is balbh é ár ngean:
Do dhíolamar teanga na nGael
ar scilling gheal an Rí,
Nach mílítheach é ár mbéal –
is ár mbeola ar easpa brí;
Do dhíolamar ár ndúchas is ár ngreann –
an chonair cham do lean.
Do thréig sí an cnoc is an gleann
teanga thréan na sean.

Mar ór ar an aiteann faoi bhláth
san Earrach mar aon bhladhm amháin
Go domhain inár gcroíthe atá –
lasair an bhua gan cháim:
Sa ghleann ina ritheann sruthán
sa smior is sa smúsach, sa chroí,
In intinn bhíogúil an ógáin
tabharfar beocht do na seansiollaí
A fhógróidh ár gcearta don lá
in aon gheal-ghaisce amháin:
Mar ór ar an aiteann faoi bhláth
faoin ngal gréine gan cháim.

Roger Casement

~

Gaelic Christianity expressed an intimacy with the Christ which was lost over the ages. (Perhaps 'the Christ' is more accurate than simply 'Christ'. It's a title, meaning 'the anointed one' and 'the' is not in use simply because there was no definite article in the language spoken by

Him, Aramaic).

In some of the shattering laments heard in the Irish tradition, Mary looks at the broken figure on the Cross and asks, 'An é sin an maicín a d'iompair mé trí ráithe?' (Is that the wee boy I carried in my womb for nine months?').

With the erosion of Gaelic civilisation (linguicide) and the rise of Anglophone Victorian bourgeois respectability, Christ became remote, inimitable. And with the loss of that intimacy, we no longer understand St Paul's instruction (Philippians 2:5-11):

"Let this mind be in you, which was also in Christ Jesus: who, being in the form of God, thought it not robbery to be equal with God."

If I have a religion at all, or world view, it is deeply coloured by Bhakti-Advaita, namely devotional non-duality. Key elements of Bhakti-Advaita can be found in all religions, especially in the mystic manifestations of Islam (Sufism), Buddhism, Judaism and Christianity itself. In that respect, I am no different, at heart, from the next man, or from Christ Himself, though He represents the perfection of humanity in so many respects.

Dogma, sectarianism and sentimental pietism can cloud and distort our view of Christ. *Christ, Gone Fishing* attempts to humanise the historical figure and see Him in the fellow in the street, sense Him in lonely spots where nothing is heard but our own breath. Of course, there's no such thing as an ordinary bloke. We are all extraordinary.

Did He ever laugh? Never, if you believe the Evangelists; but those guys were serious dudes and recent scholarship suggests that none of them actually knew Jesus in the flesh.

If we cannot see Him as Everyman, then He is no one, no more alive and real than a statue. But can we separate the quotidian from the mystic? No. Why should we? That would simply be projecting more *dvaita*, or duality, onto an overcrowded mess of multitudes: all things are wrapped in Universal Spirit, beyond Wordsworthian Pantheism, in the startling revelation of *Tat Tvam Asi,* I AM THAT.

Having said all that, it is worth stating that ekphrastic haiku have a life and energy all of their own. The landscape – in this instance, uplifting paintings by the Norwegian master Amaldus Nielsen – can trigger off spontaneous haiku utterances which easily cancel out some of the statements above, and imply or create insights 'into the life of things' (R.H. Blyth) which utterly contradict what I claim to stand for, if I stand for anything!

So what, if I contradict myself? Whitman says: 'Do I contradict myself? Very well then, I contradict myself, (I am large, I contain multitudes.'

~

Why haiku (and senryu)? Through haiku, we can often see things in a flash. Fr. Anthony de Mello, SJ, was fond of telling stories, such as this one:

"Is there such a thing as One-Minute Wisdom?"

"Certainly!" said the master.

"But . . . master, surely one minute is too brief!"

"It is fifty nine seconds too long!"

The disciple didn't know what to think.

Later, the master took him aside, and explained:

"How much time does it take to catch sight of the moon?"

"Ah! I get it! Then why all these years of spiritual endeavour, master?"

"Opening one's eyes may take a lifetime. Seeing is done in a flash!"

Why 33 haiku? Christ's years on earth. Why Nielsen? It could have been any landscape artist. However, when one looks at the lone figure standing in front of the many-branched tree in Haiku 19, one might think:

The figure could be in rapt devotion for all we know. (Tree worship, once common in Ireland, is a universal phenomenon. Christ's Cross is often referred to in Irish as *Crann na Páise,* the Passion Tree). The word *bile,* in Irish, signifies a sacred tree. Crann na hAithne, The Tree of Knowledge, is a fundamental tenet of Christian doctrine.

Nielsen's crazy tree made me think of all the various schismatic and contradictory branches of Christianity and the mindless, sectarian strife I have seen in my own country, Ireland. The haiku says: 'the teachings / and all the branches of the pine / are One.' Should not Christ's teachings all come together as One? That would be an ecumenical matter! (The phrase is from the TV sitcom, *Father Ted*).

We sometimes see deranged, fundamentalist

Christians sporting caps with the legend, 'Who would Christ bomb?' But seriously, did He ever in His brief 33 years on earth imagine Orthodox Christians, Roman Catholics, Protestants, Lutherans, Presbyterians, Methodists, Baptists, Quakers, Evangelicals, Mormons, Christian Scientists, Restorationists, Pentecostals and Charismatics, Anabaptists, Amish, Mennonites, Hutterites, Albright Brethren, Keswickians, Evening Light, Shakers, Plymouth Brethren, Irvingists, Convergence, Stone-Cambellites, P'ent'ay and all the myriad organisations such as The Legion of Mary, Opus Dei etc?. I'm sure I've missed out on a few hundred other groupings in that brief overview. Some of the best of them, such as the Diggers, are long gone! We're left, in places like the US, with a slew of money-making Bible thumpers and the hounds of Hell hot on their scent.

Who is to say whether we need the Lumpa Church, the Church of Divine Science, Psychiana and all the rest of them? Maybe we do! Let's add some colour and throw in Voodoo, Rastafarianism and whatever you're having yourself!

Oh, I don't know. I think I'll opt for Nielsen's absorbing pine tree, symbol of everlasting life!

To be fair to them, some churches are quite funny. The First Church of Awesome Works once sported a sign – maybe it still does:

> How Do We Make Holy Water? We Boil the Hell Out of It!

~

Haiku 20 suggests that all is *maya,* illusion. This may well be so. But **Haiku 24** reminds me of something wonderful that happened to Christianity, especially in the Catholic Church, namely Liberation Theology: "Master – what of this world! is there no escape from eternity?"

The influence of Liberation Theology in Northern Ireland, South America, Palestine and among the Dalit in India should not be underestimated.

> *"When I give food to the poor, they call me a saint. When I ask why so many people are poor, they call me a communist."* (Archbishop Hélder Câmara).

Haiku 28 suggests that we expect miracles and answers to our prayers when, in fact, simple meditative wordlessness rather than constantly demanding results may be a more effective method of coping with exigencies.

Indeed, the list of patron saints who are available for intercession on matters unimaginable is somewhat comic: Joseph of Cupertino, well known for feats of levitation, may be invoked by nervous air travellers, aviators, astronauts etc; the anaesthesiologist may painlessly cry out to René Goupil; arms dealers – I kid you not – will be assisted in their nefarious dealings by St. Adrian, a busy man these days; bankers may knock on the door of notorious anti-Semite Bernardine of Feltre; my namesake, Gabriel the Archangel, can be relied upon by broadcasters, ambassadors and the like; Genesius is there for clowns and comedians. Funeral directors? You guessed it, Joseph of Arimathea; Cajetan doubles up for gamblers and job seekers; the wonderfully named Christina the Astonishing will work wonders with shrinks; Ireland's Breandán (Brendan the Navigator) will pilot your vessel to safety, and so on. Even the vinegar maker has his own saint, Vincent of Saragossa, and next time you are in Valencia Cathedral, have a look at his left arm. One is left speechless.

~

May I conclude with an anecdote? A Northern Ireland journalist once interviewed me, and began with the hackneyed approach, that is to say where and when I was born. To the Advaitist, this is an impossible question, bordering on the ridiculous. Osho's epitaph always rings in his ears: never born, never died.

When I tried to clarify these basic details of life and death, before going on to discuss other less meaty matters, the journalist explained to his readers that his task had been made unimaginably difficult as Rosenstock had unexpectedly launched into an esoteric rant! I have frequently noticed that a philosophical discussion is often seen as a rant in the eyes of a WASP. (The detective novelist John Burdett tellingly reveals in a prefatory note to *The Godfather of Kathmandu* that the heart chakra of the WASP has shrunk, calamitously so. He could be right.)

~

Irony of ironies, the British – scared witless by the French Revolution – actually encouraged the revival of Advaita and Vedanta in India, seeing an otherworldliness in the Weltanschauung of the Hindu, a spiritual focus which would discourage social revolt.

And along came Gandhi. . .

Iarfhocal/Afterword

Haiku 34
cé thú féin?
cad is ainm duit?
A Thiarna atá chomh geal le seasmain!

Hold on! What's this then? Have we not established that the number of haiku in *Christ, Gone Fishing* would be 33, representing His years in this vale of tears. Yes, but what – what if there's another vale, the Vale of Kashmir and it's incredible treasure, Yusmarg, the Meadows of Jesus?
Who are you? What is Your name? Lord, white as jasmine!
What secrets lie behind **Haiku 34?**
As a wild teenager growing up in East Limerick, boarding school was the only option. What I knew about Christ–precious little – came from local clergy, then the nuns, followed by Franciscans and Spiritans. I'm afraid it wasn't enough. It wasn't a spiritual roadmap at all (though I managed to write a prize essay on the Trinity at one stage!); it was nothing more than a lifeless, spirit-less roadmap which I would later discover from the insights of Anarchists and Situationists to be a devilish roadmap devised over the centuries in cahoots with temporal

powers, the ruling classes, to keep the likes of me in check so that I would favour bankers over bank robbers, arms dealers over pacifists and so on.

I'd been given a moral compass towards good citizenry, what Guy Debord calls, 'the sun that never sets over the empire of modern passivity'. Thanks very much! Everyone had one of these, dished out like smartphones. How often this moral compass was put to use is another question.

By today's standards, my mother was pious; my father tended to be a bit of a sceptic and, furthermore, was a closet Euro-Communist and a litterateur. At boarding school, we were encouraged to read Catholic writers, G. K. Chesterton, Hilaire Belloc. Nobody bothered. My hardback copy of a George Moore's classic novel (from my father's library) was confiscated by the Dean of Studies. It was *Heloise and Abelard* (1926). I still weep because of the Dean's crime. The greatest theologian of his day had fallen in love with a nun and I had been deprived of following their shared tragedy. Books, my inner landscape, were real for me: the Dean had destroyed all that in one fell swoop and thrust me back to an unreal world, a world without romance, without soul.

Like many a teenager before and after me, I felt a vague uneasiness that gripped my mental and spiritual faculties, an uneasiness which would eventually lead me to Anarchism and Advaita, and the link between them. And then, still in my late teenage years, a miracle happened!

Haiku 34 represents a relationship I do have with Christ after all, the Universal Christ who never died on the Hill of Calvary, who returned to India, the land of His glorious apprenticeship during those "missing years", dying peacefully in old age, as countless legends inform us. One of Ireland's greatest writers, the above-mentioned George Moore, created a scandal with *The Brook Kerith,* a retelling of the Gospel published in the year of the insurrection, 1916. Ireland's literary history is a multilayered fabric!

Mary Magdalene is mentioned in **Haiku 17.** I had never come across her Gospel, though I had read Moore's classic:

> *The Savior said, All nature, all formations, all creatures exist in and with one another, and they will be resolved again into their own roots.*

Isn't that beautiful!

And so it was that I found myself, circuitously, (and found my Self) opening *Speaking of Shiva*, compiled and translated by A. K. Ramanujan (Penguin Classics), in which the refrain 'Lord, white as jasmine' repeats itself sweetly. This is Bhakti poetry. I am at home in its eternal melody.

Note from the translator, Garry Bannister:

Is léir gur deacair aistriúchán a dhéanamh ar dhán ar bith agus níos deacra fós ar Haiku. Is spléachadh tuisceana é an haiku; dúiseacht súl agus anama ar feadh soicind ghasta amháin. Chomh luath agus a lastar an solas, titimid ar ais arís isteach sa dorchdas saolta. Is é ginias Rosenstock gur féidir leis na soilse uile a lasadh dúinn le cúpla focal tofa cuí. Uaireanta éiríonn leis an aistriúchán breith ar mhistéir éalaitheach an haiku nó a bheith ina scáthán ar aga an imléargais anama ach uaireanta eile, ní bhíonn sa Bhéarla ach creatlach lom cré den eispearas úd atá nochta go neamhbhalbh sa Ghaeilge. Sin ráite, is cnuasach cumasach álainn eile é seo ó pheann mháistirfhile na fealsúnachta spioradálta, Gabriel Rosenstock.

Other ekphrastic haiku books by the author include:

Iontas na nIontas (Irish & English glossary, with Christian iconography)
ISBN: 978-1906982812

The Stars are His Bones (found haiku from the Upanishads)
Photographs by Debiprasad Mukherjee
ISBN-10: 0893047082
ISBN-13: 978-0893047085

The Barking of Waves/Tafann na dTonn
Photographs by Ron Rosenstock
ISBN-10: 1851323279
ISBN-13: 978-185132327

Judgement Day (bilingual, with Dadaist work by Karl Waldmann)
ISBN: 978-0993421785

Antlered Stag of Dawn (Irish, English, Japanese & Scots)
Inspired by a photo of the Very Venerable Chögyam Trungpa in Highland Regalia).
ISBN: 978-0992723897

Stillness of Crows, bilingual
Artwork by Ohara Koson
ISBN-10 : 1724919261
ISBN-13: 978-1724919267

Angelic Flights
Photographs by Kon Markogiannis
ISBN-10: 0893047090
ISBN-13: 978-0893047092

Rare Times
Photographs by Jason Symes
ASIN: B06X1B81Y2

Orpheus in the Underpass
Photographs by Ross McKessock
ISBN-10: 1912111705
ISBN-13: 978-1912111701

Silver Birches
Irish, Japanese, English, French, Greek
ASIN: B0833KLD81

A Sweater for the Tayfel
Bilingual haiku in response to artwork by Issacher Ber Rybek (Ukraine) (Buttonhook Press, 2022)

www.ingramcontent.com/pod-product-compliance
Lightning Source LLC
Chambersburg PA
CBHW061234070526
44584CB00030B/4112